Easter Coloring Books For Kids :

2016 Easter Coloring Pages For Hours Of Fun For Children Of All Ages

Zen Journal Team

Coloring Pages By Zen Volume 1

Published by Sun Bubbles Publishing in 2016
First edition; First Printing

Design and writing ©2016 Zen Journal Team

SunBubblesPublishing.com

All rights reserved. No part of this book may be reproduced or transmitted in any form or by any means, including but not limited to information storage and retrieval systems, electronic, mechanical, photocopy, recording, etc. withoutwritten permission from the copyright holder.

ISBN 978-1-944230-12-8

THIS BOOK BELONGS TO:

_____

This is a Bleed Through Page If You Are Using a Coloring Marker or Pen! *Find Other Great Titles By Zen Journal Team. Search on Your Favorite Book Retailer* **Amazon.Com | Barnes & Noble (BN.Com) | Books A Million (BAM.Com)**

This is a Bleed Through Page If You Are Using a Coloring Marker or Pen! *Find Other Great Titles By Zen Journal Team. Search on Your Favorite Book Retailer* **Amazon.Com I Barnes & Noble (BN.Com) I Books A Million (BAM.Com)**

This is a Bleed Through Page If You Are Using a Coloring Marker or Pen! Find Other Great Titles By Zen Journal Team. Search on Your Favorite Book Retailer **Amazon.Com I Barnes & Noble (BN.Com) I Books A Million (BAM.Com)**

This is a Bleed Through Page If You Are Using a Coloring Marker or Pen! *Find Other Great Titles By Zen Journal Team. Search on Your Favorite Book Retailer* **Amazon.Com I Barnes & Noble (BN.Com) I Books A Million (BAM.Com)**

This is a Bleed Through Page If You Are Using a Coloring Marker or Pen! *Find Other Great Titles By Zen Journal Team. Search on Your Favorite Book Retailer* **Amazon.Com | Barnes & Noble (BN.Com) | Books A Million (BAM.Com)**

This is a Bleed Through Page If You Are Using a Coloring Marker or Pen! *Find Other Great Titles By Zen Journal Team. Search on Your Favorite Book Retailer* **Amazon.Com l Barnes & Noble (BN.Com) l Books A Million (BAM.Com)**

This is a Bleed Through Page If You Are Using a Coloring Marker or Pen! *Find Other Great Titles By Zen Journal Team. Search on Your Favorite Book Retailer* **Amazon.Com | Barnes & Noble (BN.Com) | Books A Million (BAM.Com)**

This is a Bleed Through Page If You Are Using a Coloring Marker or Pen! *Find Other Great Titles By Zen Journal Team. Search on Your Favorite Book Retailer* **Amazon.Com I Barnes & Noble (BN.Com) I Books A Million (BAM.Com)**

This is a Bleed Through Page If You Are Using a Coloring Marker or Pen! *Find Other Great Titles By Zen Journal Team. Search on Your Favorite Book Retailer* **Amazon.Com | Barnes & Noble (BN.Com) | Books A Million (BAM.Com)**

This is a Bleed Through Page If You Are Using a Coloring Marker or Pen! *Find Other Great Titles By Zen Journal Team. Search on Your Favorite Book Retailer* **Amazon.Com | Barnes & Noble (BN.Com) | Books A Million (BAM.Com)**

This is a Bleed Through Page If You Are Using a Coloring Marker or Pen! *Find Other Great Titles By Zen Journal Team. Search on Your Favorite Book Retailer* **Amazon.Com | Barnes & Noble (BN.Com) | Books A Million (BAM.Com)**

This is a Bleed Through Page If You Are Using a Coloring Marker or Pen! *Find Other Great Titles By Zen Journal Team. Search on Your Favorite Book Retailer* Amazon.Com | Barnes & Noble (BN.Com) | Books A Million (BAM.Com)

This is a Bleed Through Page If You Are Using a Coloring Marker or Pen! *Find Other Great Titles By Zen Journal Team. Search on Your Favorite Book Retailer* **Amazon.Com | Barnes & Noble (BN.Com) | Books A Million (BAM.Com)**

This is a Bleed Through Page If You Are Using a Coloring Marker or Pen! *Find Other Great Titles By Zen Journal Team. Search on Your Favorite Book Retailer* **Amazon.Com l Barnes & Noble (BN.Com) l Books A Million (BAM.Com)**

This is a Bleed Through Page If You Are Using a Coloring Marker or Pen! *Find Other Great Titles By Zen Journal Team. Search on Your Favorite Book Retailer* **Amazon.Com I Barnes & Noble (BN.Com) I Books A Million (BAM.Com)**

This is a Bleed Through Page If You Are Using a Coloring Marker or Pen! *Find Other Great Titles By Zen Journal Team. Search on Your Favorite Book Retailer* Amazon.Com | Barnes & Noble (BN.Com) | Books A Million (BAM.Com)

This is a Bleed Through Page If You Are Using a Coloring Marker or Pen! Find Other Great Titles By Zen Journal Team. Search on Your Favorite Book Retailer **Amazon.Com I Barnes & Noble (BN.Com) I Books A Million (BAM.Com)**

This is a Bleed Through Page If You Are Using a Coloring Marker or Pen! *Find Other Great Titles By Zen Journal Team. Search on Your Favorite Book Retailer* **Amazon.Com | Barnes & Noble (BN.Com) | Books A Million (BAM.Com)**

This is a Bleed Through Page If You Are Using a Coloring Marker or Pen! *Find Other Great Titles By Zen Journal Team. Search on Your Favorite Book Retailer* Amazon.Com | Barnes & Noble (BN.Com) | Books A Million (BAM.Com)

This is a Bleed Through Page If You Are Using a Coloring Marker or Pen! *Find Other Great Titles By Zen Journal Team. Search on Your Favorite Book Retailer* **Amazon.Com | Barnes & Noble (BN.Com) | Books A Million (BAM.Com)**

This is a Bleed Through Page If You Are Using a Coloring Marker or Pen! Find Other Great Titles By Zen Journal Team. Search on Your Favorite Book Retailer Amazon.Com I Barnes & Noble (BN.Com) I Books A Million (BAM.Com)

This is a Bleed Through Page If You Are Using a Coloring Marker or Pen! *Find Other Great Titles By Zen Journal Team. Search on Your Favorite Book Retailer* **Amazon.Com I Barnes & Noble (BN.Com) I Books A Million (BAM.Com)**

This is a Bleed Through Page If You Are Using a Coloring Marker or Pen! *Find Other Great Titles By Zen Journal Team. Search on Your Favorite Book Retailer* **Amazon.Com | Barnes & Noble (BN.Com) | Books A Million (BAM.Com)**

This is a Bleed Through Page If You Are Using a Coloring Marker or Pen! *Find Other Great Titles By Zen Journal Team. Search on Your Favorite Book Retailer*
Amazon.Com I Barnes & Noble (BN.Com) I Books A Million (BAM.Com)

This is a Bleed Through Page If You Are Using a Coloring Marker or Pen! *Find Other Great Titles By Zen Journal Team. Search on Your Favorite Book Retailer*
Amazon.Com | Barnes & Noble (BN.Com) | Books A Million (BAM.Com)

This is a Bleed Through Page If You Are Using a Coloring Marker or Pen! *Find Other Great Titles By Zen Journal Team. Search on Your Favorite Book Retailer* **Amazon.Com | Barnes & Noble (BN.Com) | Books A Million (BAM.Com)**

This is a Bleed Through Page If You Are Using a Coloring Marker or Pen! Find Other Great Titles By Zen Journal Team. Search on Your Favorite Book Retailer Amazon.Com I Barnes & Noble (BN.Com) I Books A Million (BAM.Com)

This is a Bleed Through Page If You Are Using a Coloring Marker or Pen! *Find Other Great Titles By Zen Journal Team. Search on Your Favorite Book Retailer* **Amazon.Com I Barnes & Noble (BN.Com) I Books A Million (BAM.Com)**

This is a Bleed Through Page If You Are Using a Coloring Marker or Pen! *Find Other Great Titles By Zen Journal Team. Search on Your Favorite Book Retailer* **Amazon.Com | Barnes & Noble (BN.Com) | Books A Million (BAM.Com)**

This is a Bleed Through Page If You Are Using a Coloring Marker or Pen! Find Other Great Titles By Zen Journal Team. Search on Your Favorite Book Retailer **Amazon.Com I Barnes & Noble (BN.Com) I Books A Million (BAM.Com)**

This is a Bleed Through Page If You Are Using a Coloring Marker or Pen! *Find Other Great Titles By Zen Journal Team. Search on Your Favorite Book Retailer* **Amazon.Com | Barnes & Noble (BN.Com) | Books A Million (BAM.Com)**

This is a Bleed Through Page If You Are Using a Coloring Marker or Pen! *Find Other Great Titles By Zen Journal Team. Search on Your Favorite Book Retailer*
Amazon.Com | Barnes & Noble (BN.Com) | Books A Million (BAM.Com)

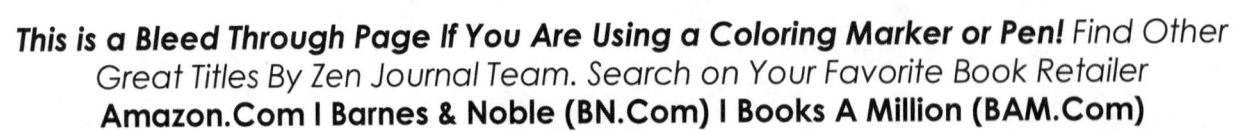

Put a pattern on the egg.

This is a Bleed Through Page If You Are Using a Coloring Marker or Pen! Find Other Great Titles By Zen Journal Team. Search on Your Favorite Book Retailer Amazon.Com l Barnes & Noble (BN.Com) l Books A Million (BAM.Com)

This is a Bleed Through Page If You Are Using a Coloring Marker or Pen! Find Other Great Titles By Zen Journal Team. Search on Your Favorite Book Retailer
Amazon.Com I Barnes & Noble (BN.Com) I Books A Million (BAM.Com)

This is a Bleed Through Page If You Are Using a Coloring Marker or Pen! *Find Other Great Titles By Zen Journal Team. Search on Your Favorite Book Retailer* **Amazon.Com | Barnes & Noble (BN.Com) | Books A Million (BAM.Com)**

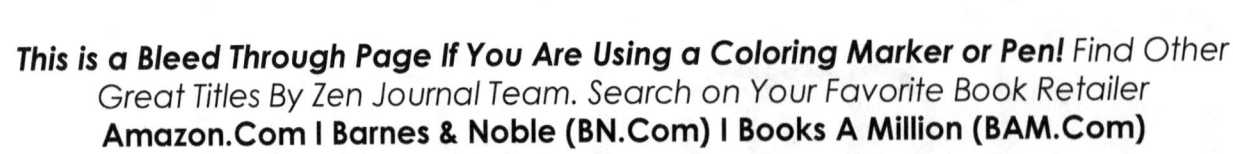

This is a Bleed Through Page If You Are Using a Coloring Marker or Pen! *Find Other Great Titles By Zen Journal Team. Search on Your Favorite Book Retailer* **Amazon.Com I Barnes & Noble (BN.Com) I Books A Million (BAM.Com)**

This is a Bleed Through Page If You Are Using a Coloring Marker or Pen! *Find Other Great Titles By Zen Journal Team. Search on Your Favorite Book Retailer* **Amazon.Com | Barnes & Noble (BN.Com) | Books A Million (BAM.Com)**

This is a Bleed Through Page If You Are Using a Coloring Marker or Pen! Find Other Great Titles By Zen Journal Team. Search on Your Favorite Book Retailer **Amazon.Com | Barnes & Noble (BN.Com) | Books A Million (BAM.Com)**

This is a Bleed Through Page If You Are Using a Coloring Marker or Pen! *Find Other Great Titles By Zen Journal Team. Search on Your Favorite Book Retailer* **Amazon.Com I Barnes & Noble (BN.Com) I Books A Million (BAM.Com)**

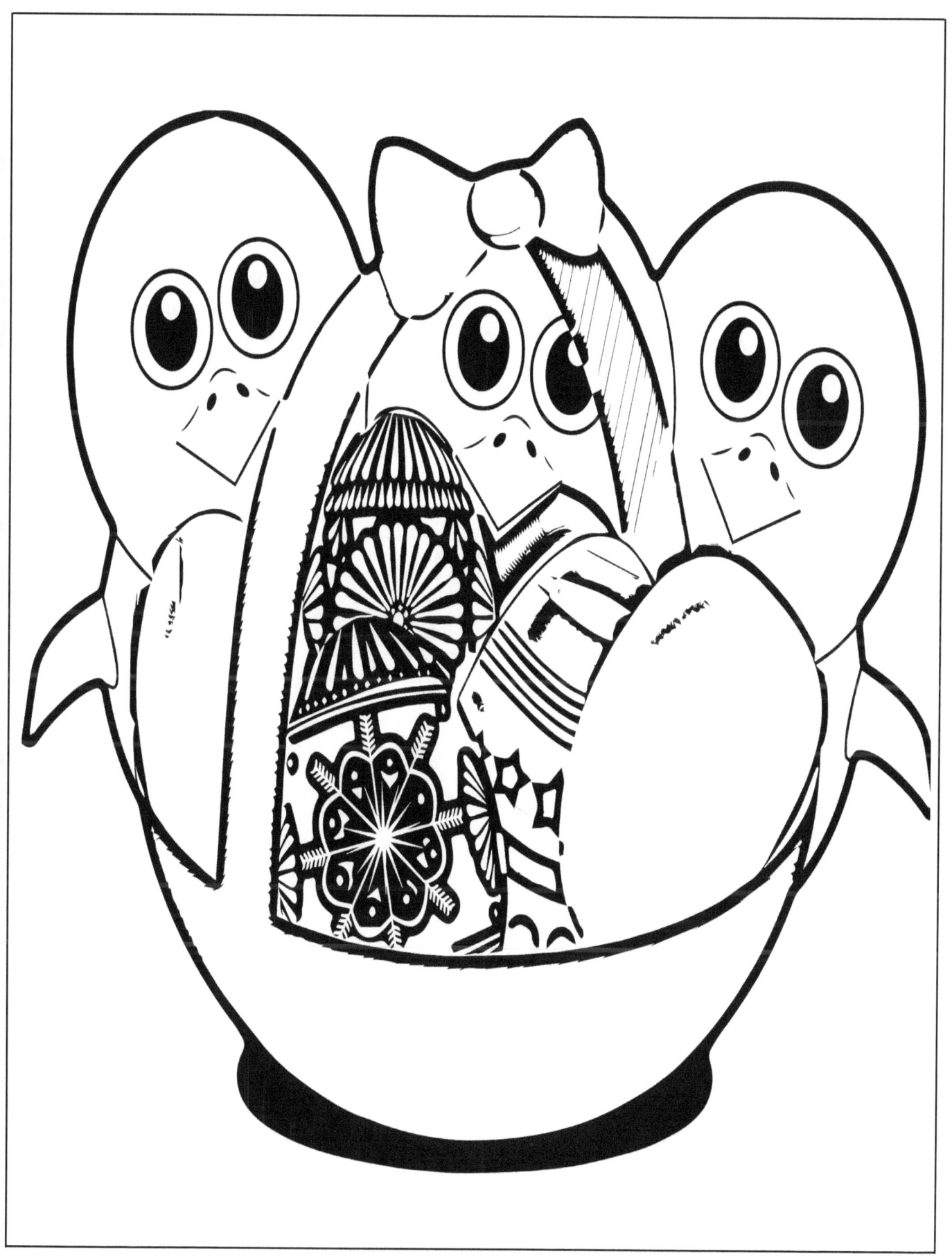

This is a Bleed Through Page If You Are Using a Coloring Marker or Pen! *Find Other Great Titles By Zen Journal Team. Search on Your Favorite Book Retailer* **Amazon.Com I Barnes & Noble (BN.Com) I Books A Million (BAM.Com)**

This is a Bleed Through Page If You Are Using a Coloring Marker or Pen! Find Other Great Titles By Zen Journal Team. Search on Your Favorite Book Retailer Amazon.Com I Barnes & Noble (BN.Com) I Books A Million (BAM.Com)

About The Zen Journal Team

The Zen Journal Team prides itself on producing quality themed coloring books for adults and children alike. This latest title "Easter Coloring Books For Kids" is a children's coloring book that features beautiful kid friendly coloring in designs of some of our favorite Easter characters.

In 'Easter Coloring Books For Kids"you will find pictures of Easter Bunnies, chocolate eggs, cute baby chicks, farm animals, Easter scenes and much more that will keep even the most active mind busy coloring in for hours!

Happy Easter To Everyone!

Visit us online to download free Coloring Pages and to see our full range of themed Coloring Books:

www.ZenArtworkMandalas.com

www.ingramcontent.com/pod-product-compliance
Lightning Source LLC
Chambersburg PA
CBHW081017040426

42444CB00014B/3251